I0405087

midlife crisis penis

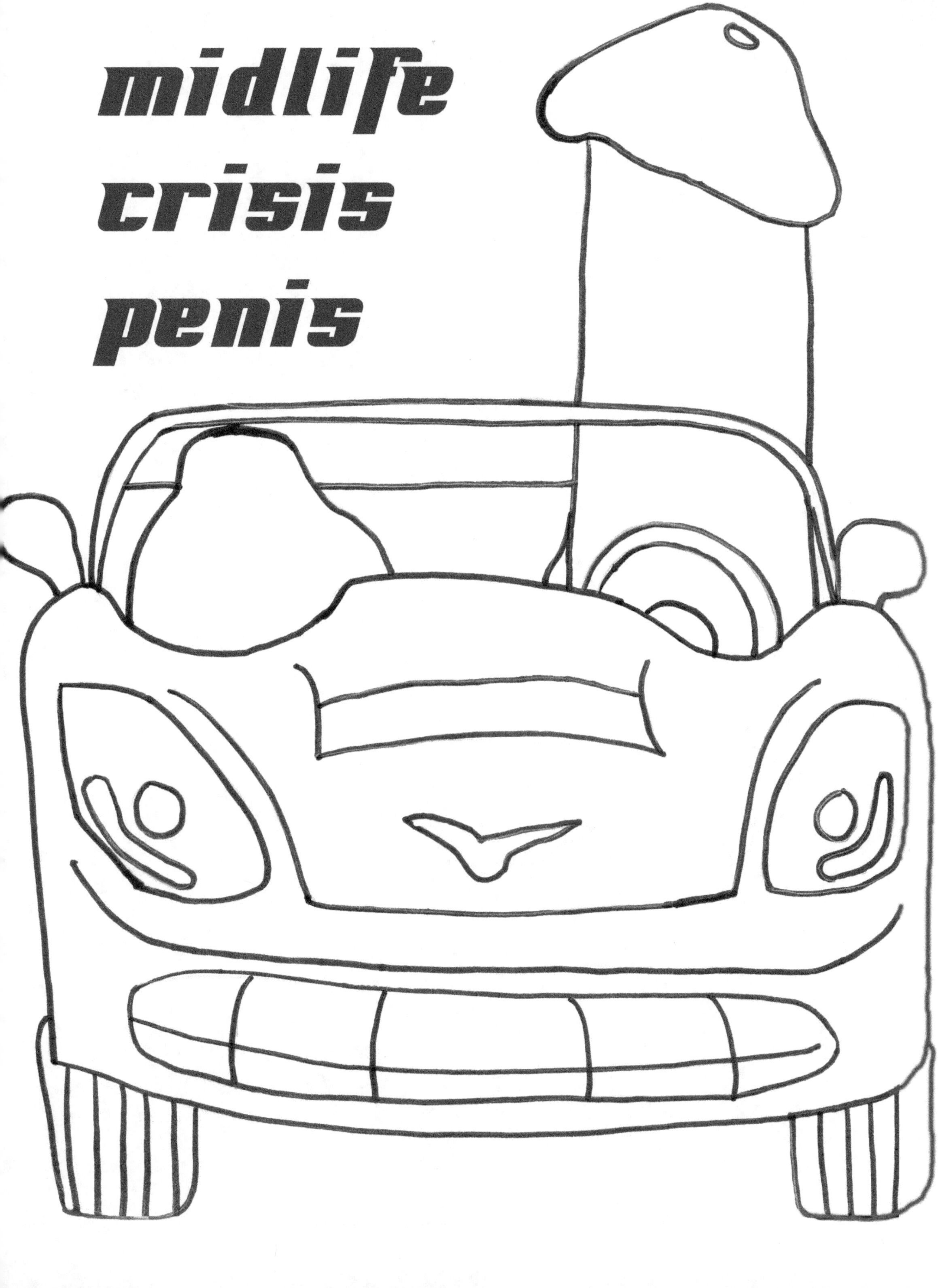

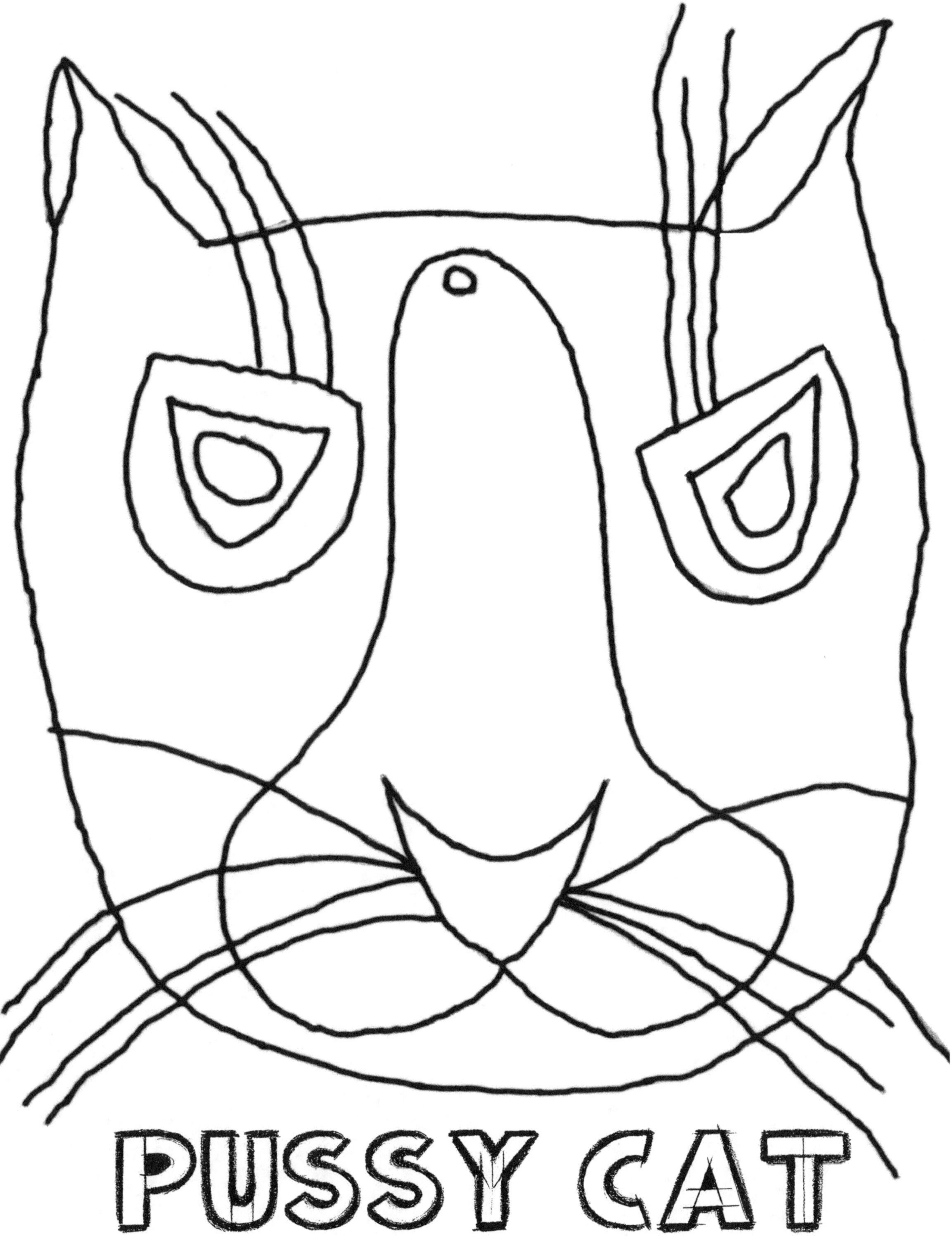

PUSSY CAT

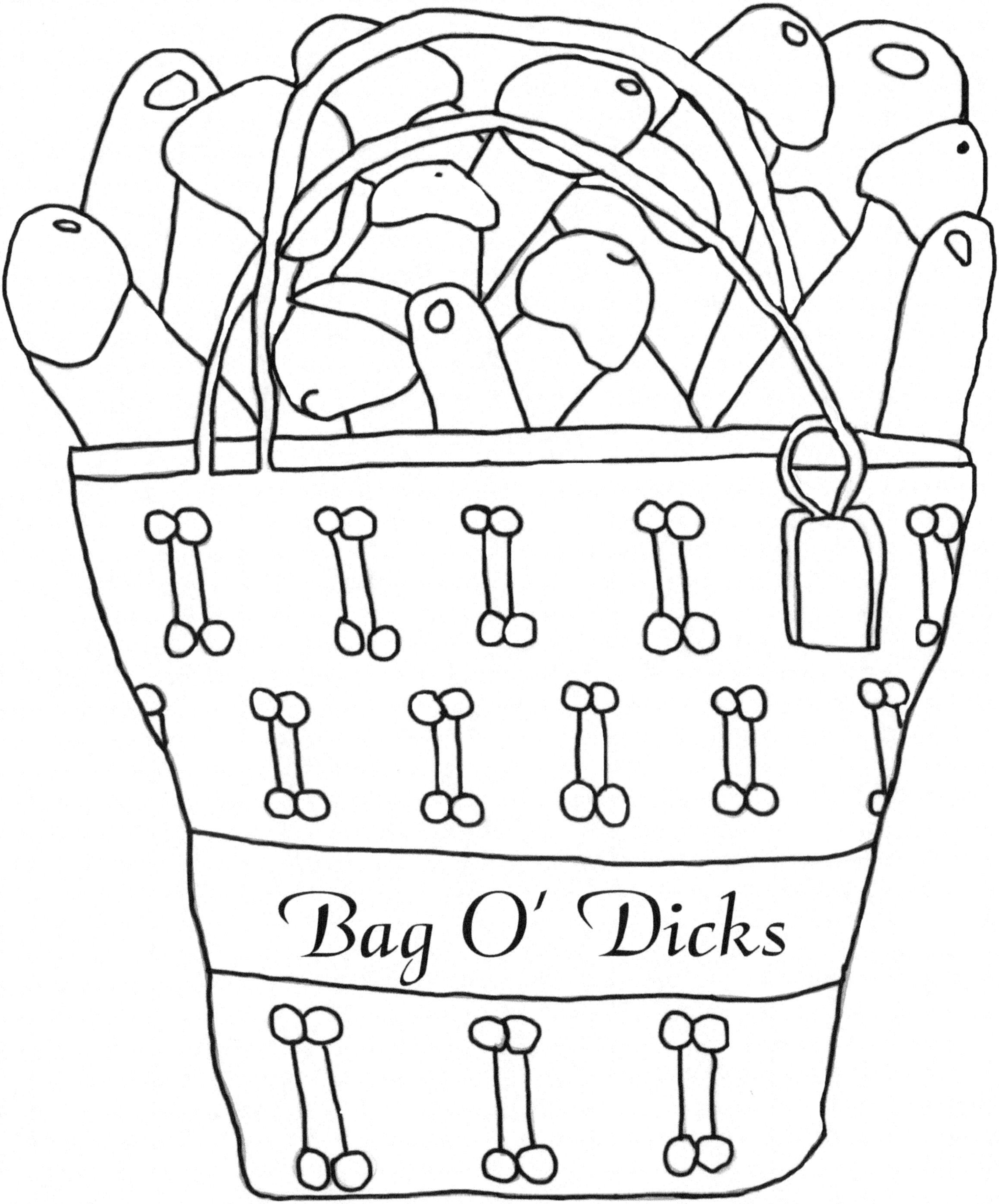
Bag O' Dicks

Penis Cornucopia

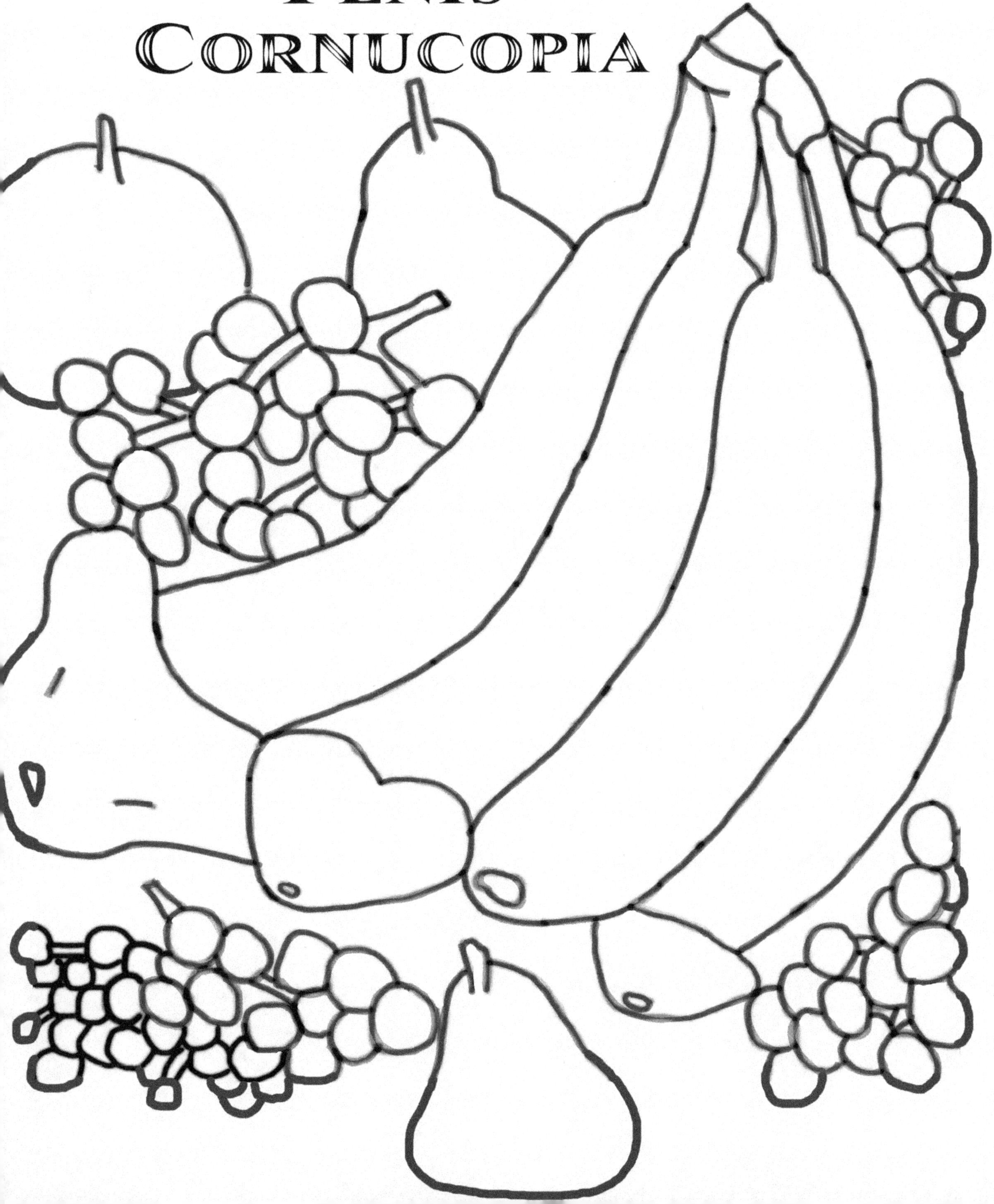

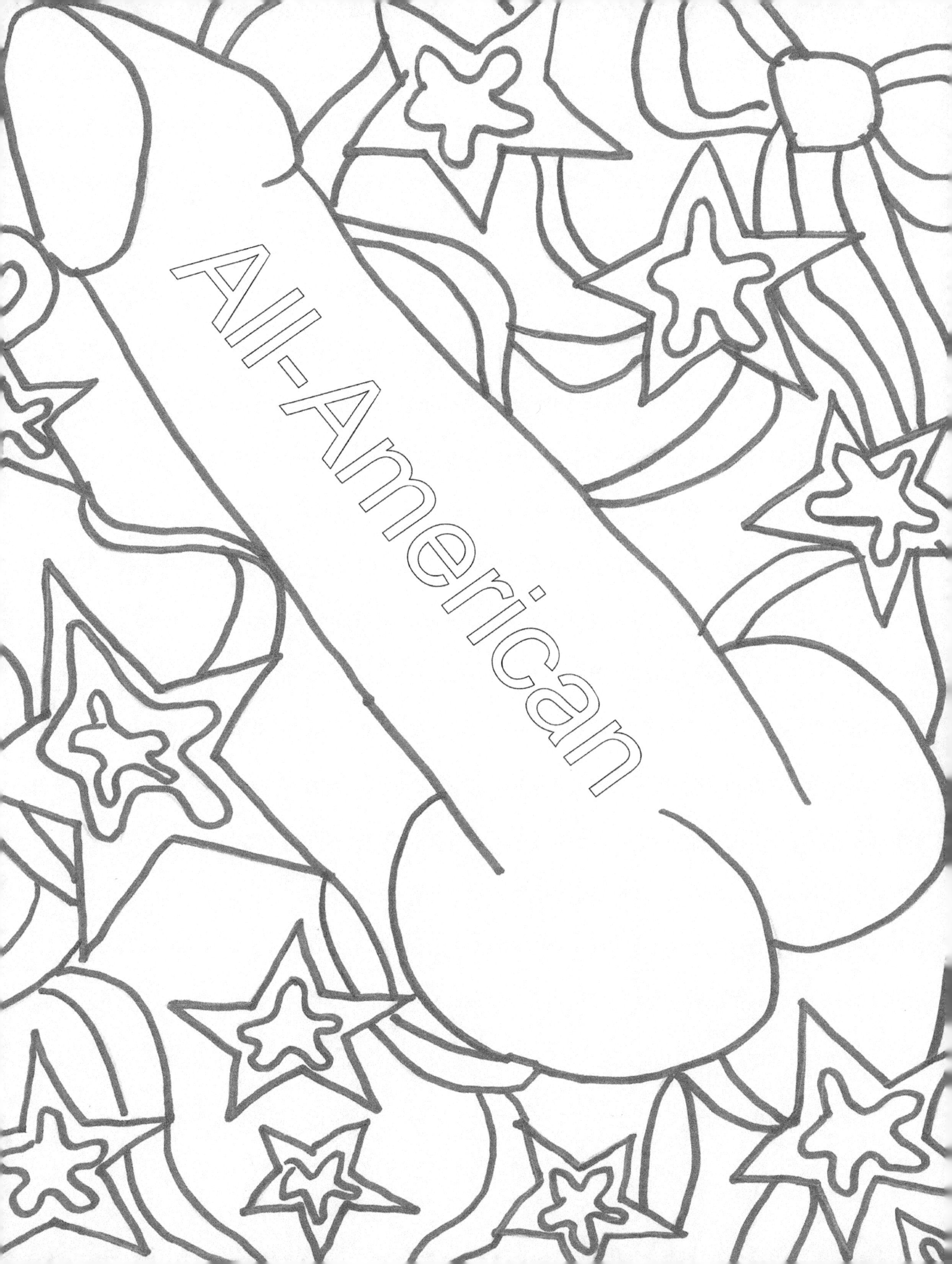
All-American

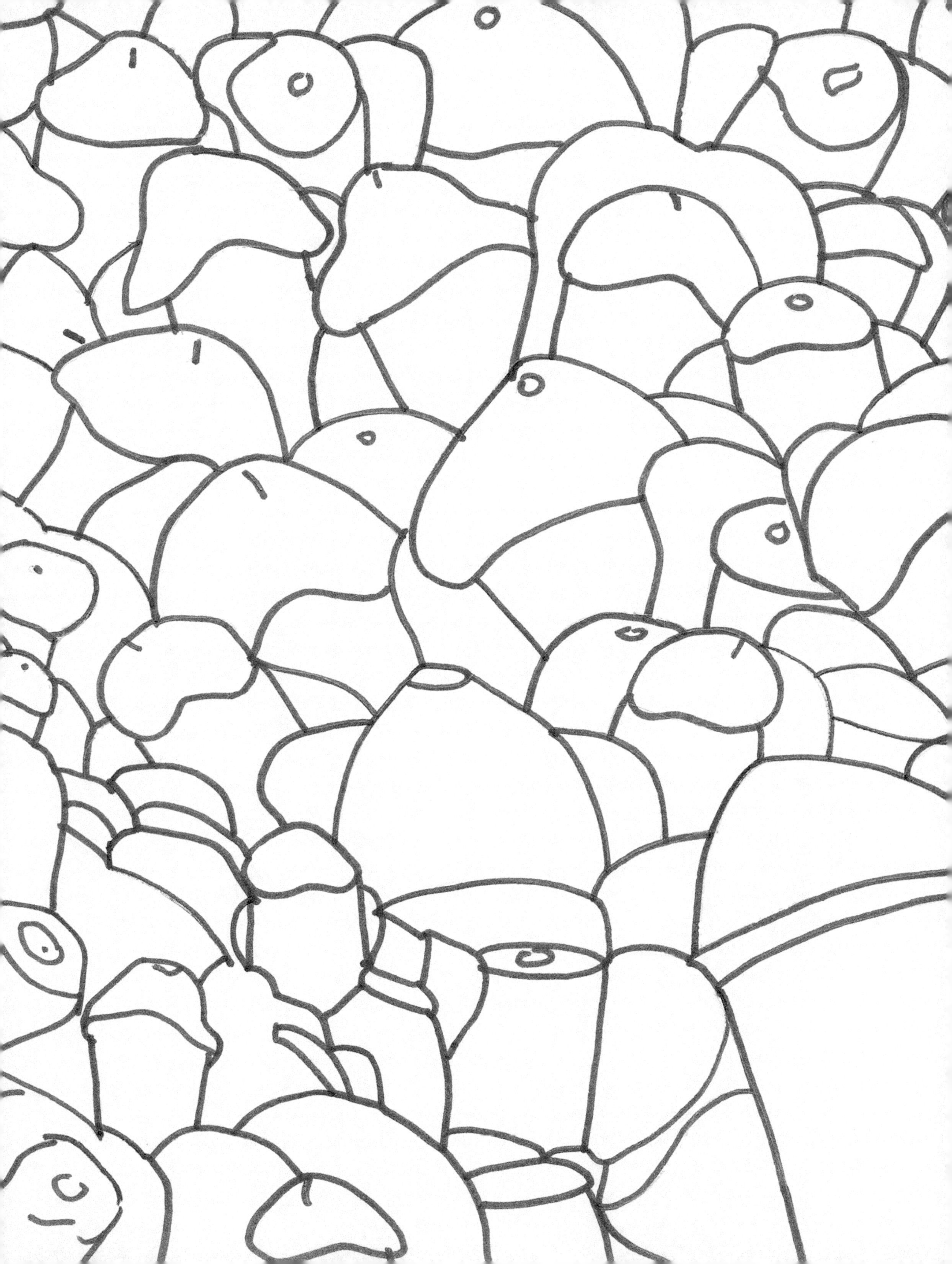

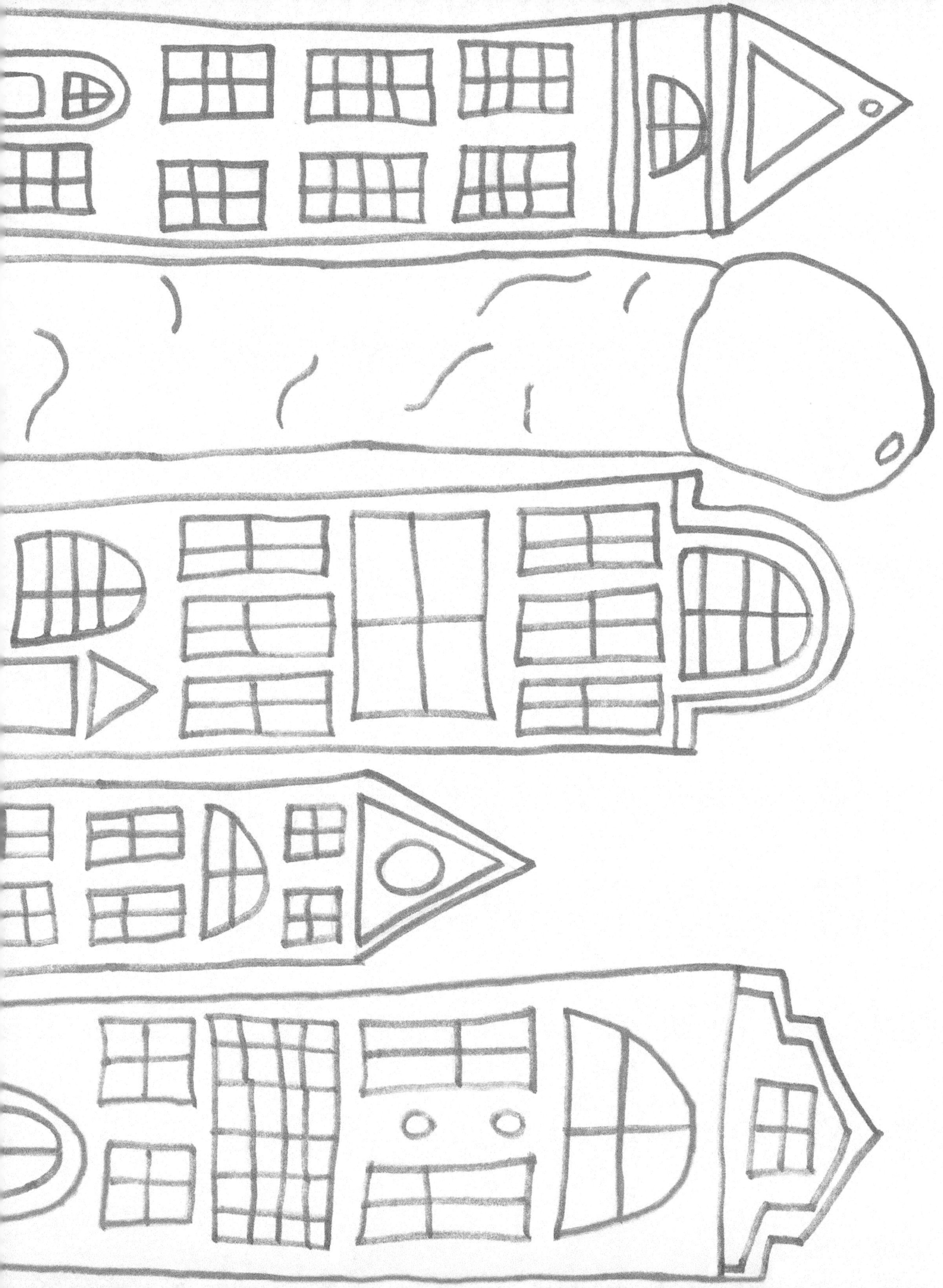

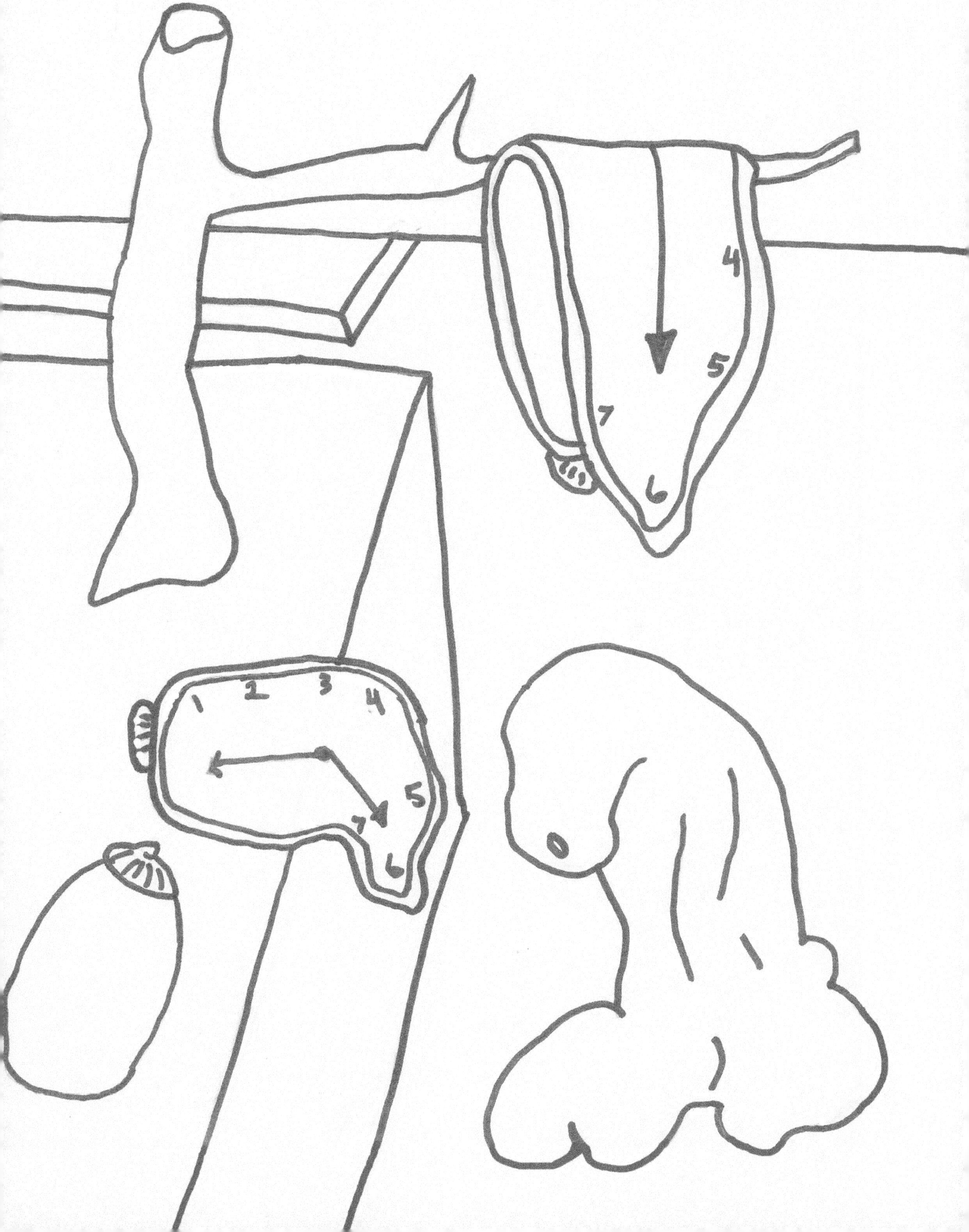

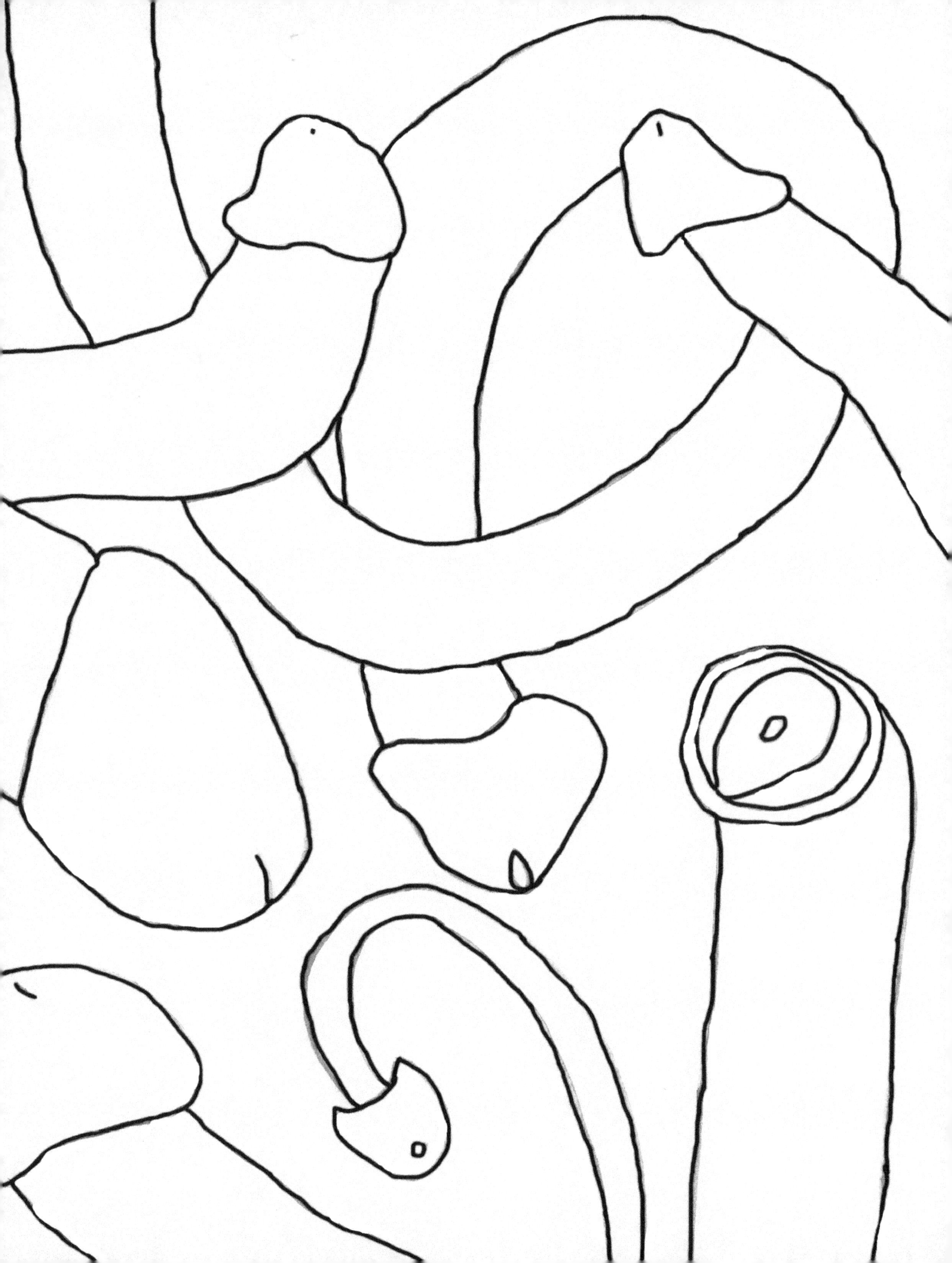

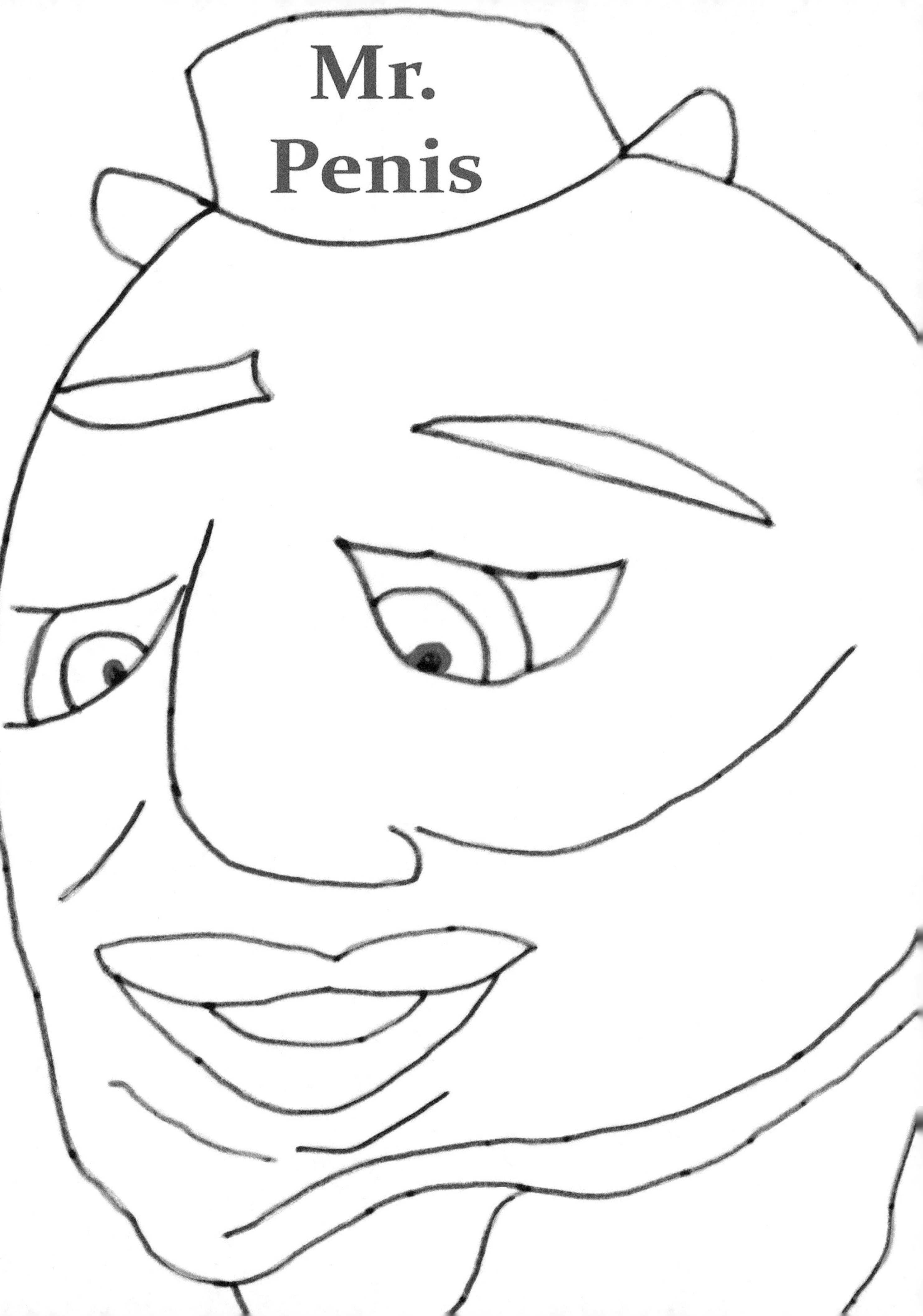
Mr.
Penis

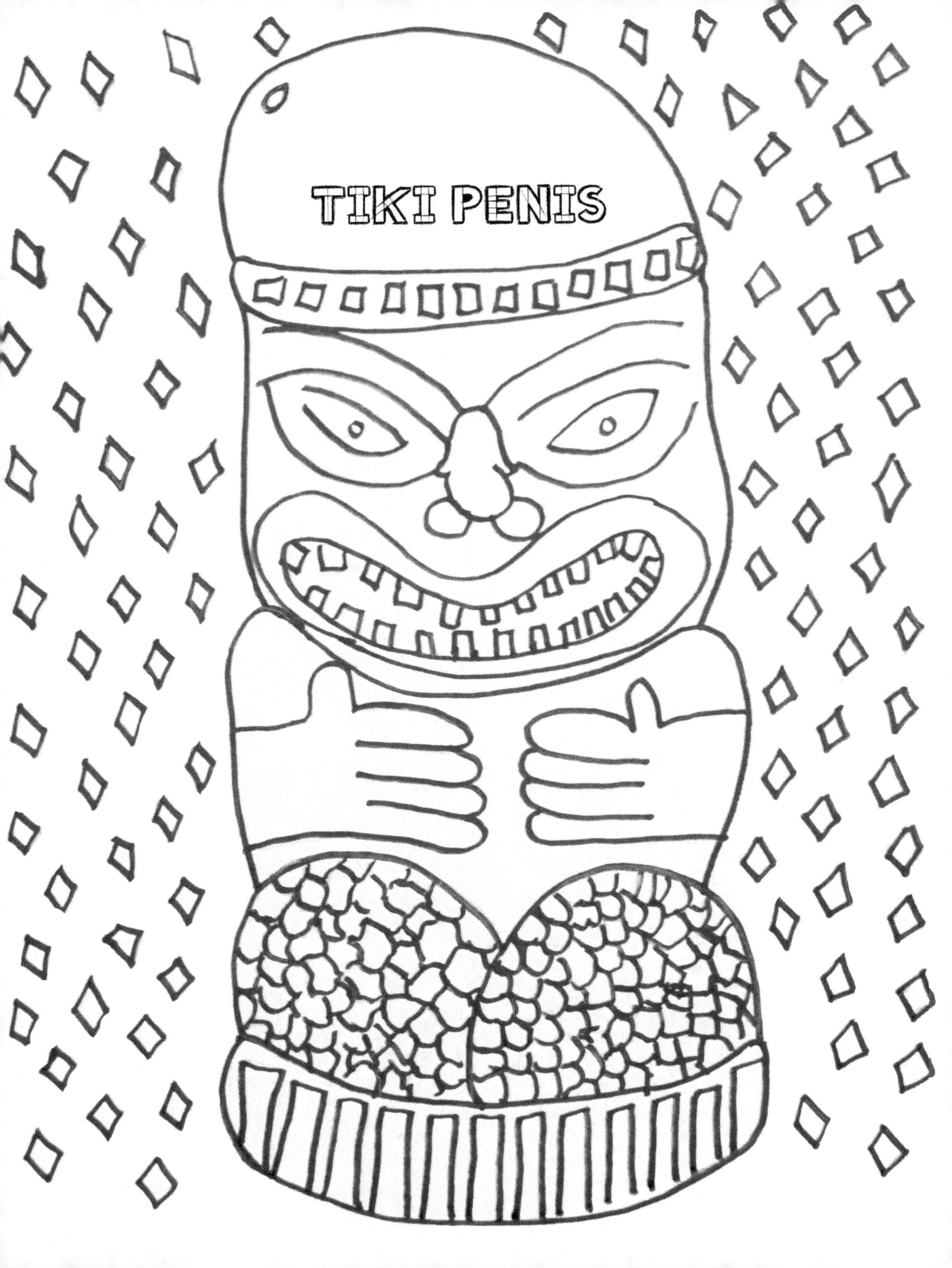
TIKI PENIS

You're
So
Vein

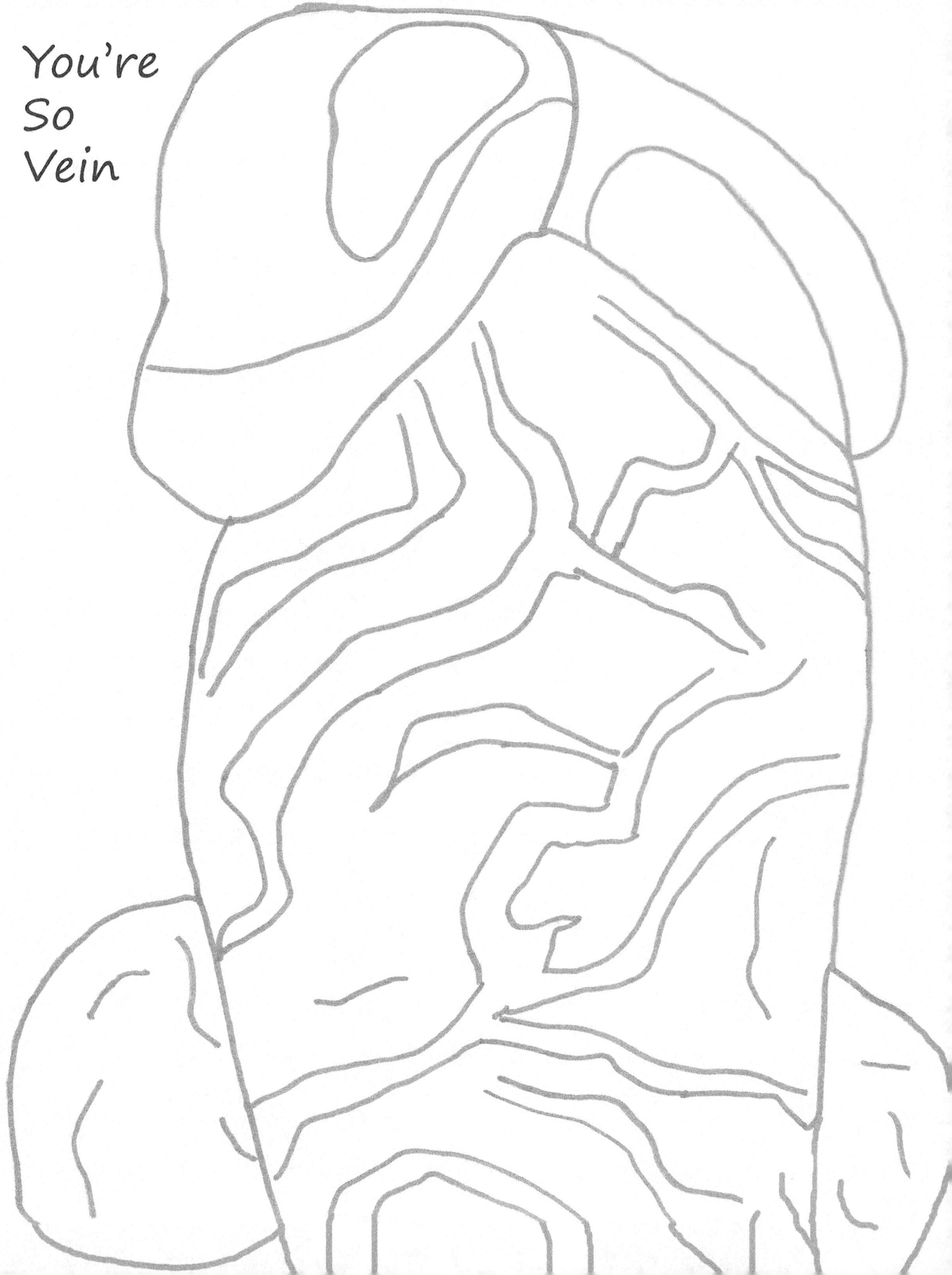

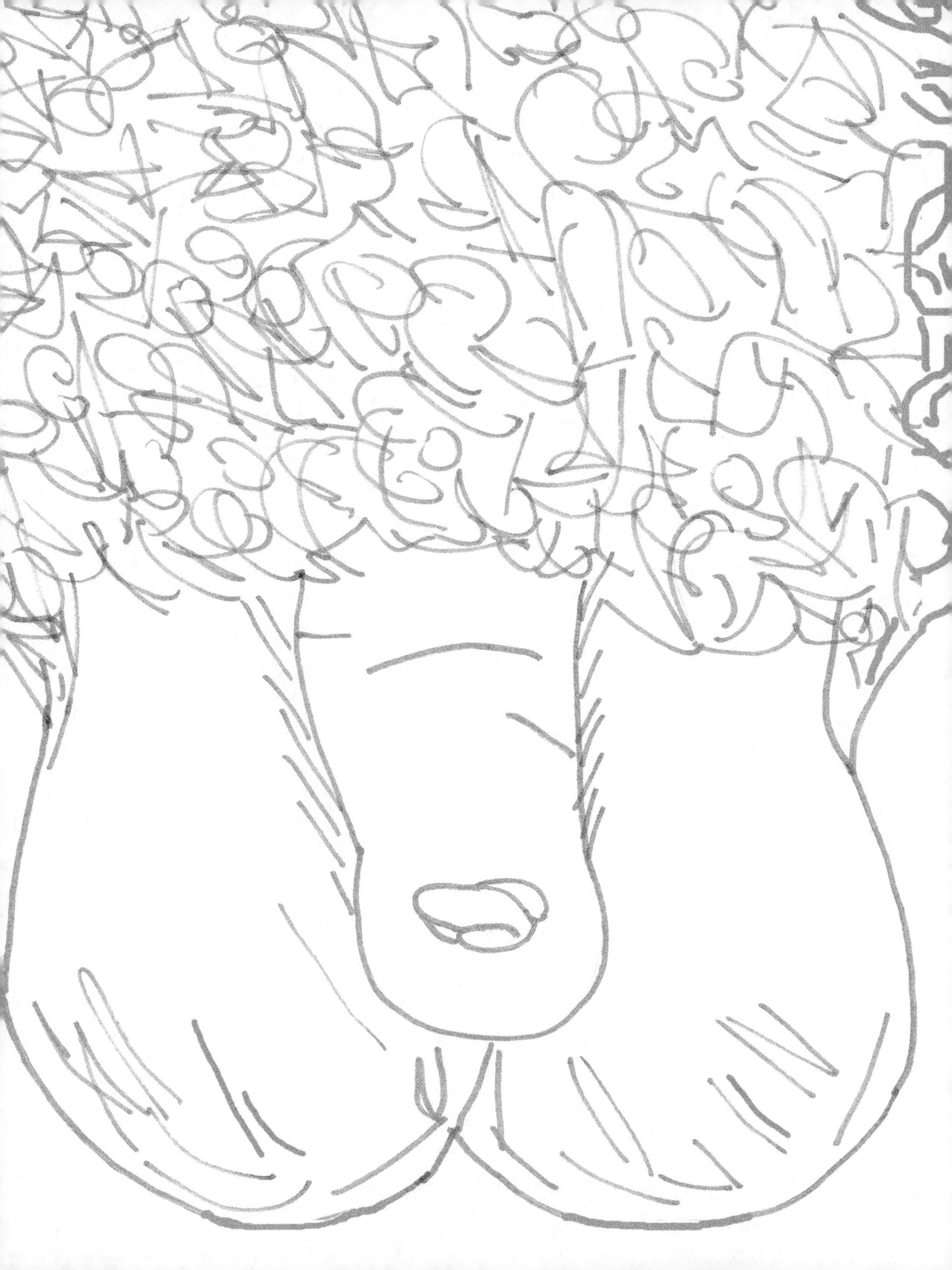

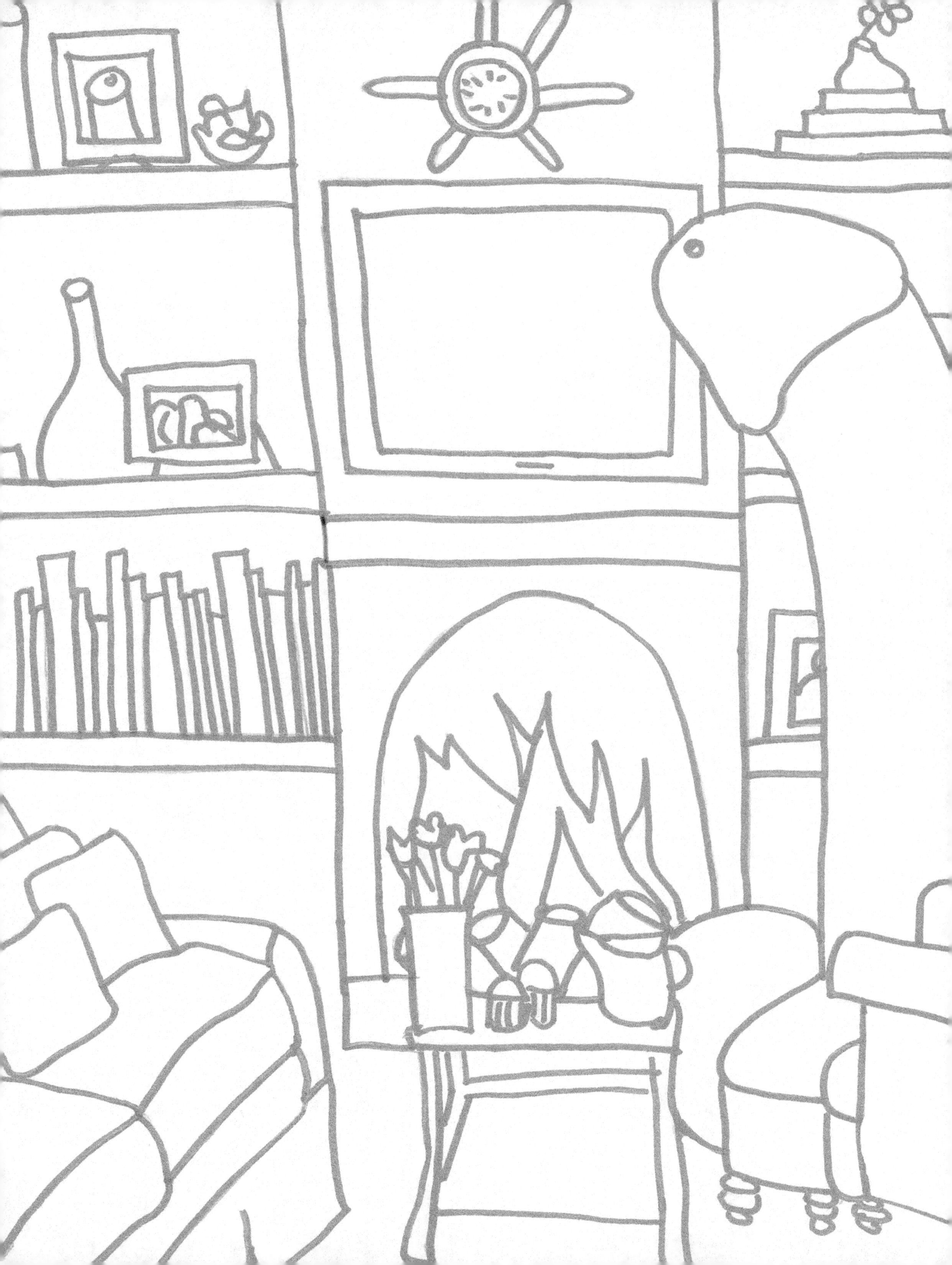

www.ingramcontent.com/pod-product-compliance
Lightning Source LLC
Chambersburg PA
CBHW080532190526
45169CB00008B/3128
9781537072180